WAKE UP! WAKE UP!

起床了!

Kathleen R. Seaton 著

姚 紅 繪

The clock *shouted: "Wake up! Wake up!"

*為生字，請參照生字表

"Time to *get up!" said Mother.

"Ben! Ben! Time for school," said Big Sister.

"One *more minute," I told her.

"Get out of bed! Get ready for school,"

Big Brother said.

"Just one more minute," I said.

"Time to wake up!" said Little Sister shaking me.

" *Go away!" I said.

"Get up! Get up!" Little Brother shouted in my ear.

"Not now!" I cried.

"Wake up," *called Grandfather.

"Wake up! Time for breakfast," called Grandmother.

"Get out of bed right now!" shouted Father.

"Okay, okay," I said.

"Brush your teeth," said Mother.

"Wash your face," said Big Sister.

"*Put on your *clothes!" said Father.

"Hurry. Eat your breakfast!" said Little Sister.

"Put on your shoes!" Big Brother said.

"Put on your coat," Grandfather said.

"Go to school. Don't be late," Little Brother said.

"He forgot his books!" cried Big Sister.

"You forgot your books," said Mother.

16

"Hurry! You'll be late for school," Father said.

"Wake up! Wake up!" my *classmates *yelled.

"Wake up! Time for math," my teacher said.

20

"Wake up! Time for lunch," my friends said.

"Wake up! Time to clean up," my *principal said.

"Wake up! Time to go home," my teacher said.

"I'm *awake!" I shouted, running to my home.

生_{ㄕㄥ}字_{ㄗˋ}表_{ㄅㄧㄠˇ}

wake [wek] v. 睡_{ㄕㄨㄟˋ}醒_{ㄒㄧㄥˇ}

wake up　起_{ㄑㄧˇ}床_{ㄔㄨㄤˊ}

p.2

shout [ʃaut] v. 發_{ㄈㄚ}出_{ㄔㄨ}很_{ㄏㄣˇ}大_{ㄉㄚˋ}的_{ㄉㄜ}聲_{ㄕㄥ}音_{ㄧㄣ}

p.3

get up　起_{ㄑㄧˇ}床_{ㄔㄨㄤˊ}

p.4

more [mor] adj. 更_{ㄍㄥˋ}多_{ㄉㄨㄛ}的_{ㄉㄜ}；另_{ㄌㄧㄥˋ}外_{ㄨㄞˋ}的_{ㄉㄜ}

p.8

go away　走_{ㄗㄡˇ}開_{ㄎㄞ}

p.10

call [kɔl] v. 喊_{ㄏㄢˇ}叫_{ㄐㄧㄠˋ}

p.13

put on　穿_{ㄔㄨㄢ}、戴_{ㄉㄞˋ}（衣_ㄧ物_{ㄨˋ}）

clothes [kloz] n. 衣_ㄧ服_{ㄈㄨˊ}

p.19

classmate [ˋklæs,met] n. 同_{ㄊㄨㄥˊ}班_{ㄅㄢ}同_{ㄊㄨㄥˊ}學_{ㄒㄩㄝˊ}

yell [jɛl] v. 叫_{ㄐㄧㄠˋ}喊_{ㄏㄢˇ}

p.22

principal [ˋprɪnsəpl] n. 校_{ㄒㄧㄠˋ}長_{ㄓㄤˇ}

p.24

awake [əˋwek] adj. 清_{ㄑㄧㄥ}醒_{ㄒㄧㄥˇ}的_{ㄉㄜ}

adj.= 形_{ㄒㄧㄥˊ}容_{ㄖㄨㄥˊ}詞_ˊ，n.= 名_{ㄇㄧㄥˊ}詞_ˊ，v.= 動_{ㄉㄨㄥˋ}詞_ˊ

起ㄑ一ˇ床ㄔㄨㄤˊ了ㄌㄜ˙！

p.2-3

鬧ㄋㄠˋ鐘ㄓㄨㄥ響ㄒ一ㄤˇ起ㄑ一ˇ：「起ㄑ一ˇ床ㄔㄨㄤˊ了ㄌㄜ˙！起ㄑ一ˇ床ㄔㄨㄤˊ了ㄌㄜ˙！」

媽ㄇㄚ媽ㄇㄚ說ㄕㄨㄛ：「該ㄍㄞ起ㄑ一ˇ床ㄔㄨㄤˊ了ㄌㄜ˙！」

p.4-5

姊ㄐ一ㄝˇ姊ㄐ一ㄝˇ說ㄕㄨㄛ：「小ㄒ一ㄠˇ班ㄅㄢ！小ㄒ一ㄠˇ班ㄅㄢ！要一ㄠˋ上ㄕㄤˋ學ㄒ一ㄝˊ囉ㄌㄡ！」

我ㄨㄛˇ對ㄉㄨㄟˋ她ㄊㄚ說ㄕㄨㄛ：「再ㄗㄞˋ一ㄧ分ㄈㄣ鐘ㄓㄨㄥ。」

p.6-7

哥ㄍㄜ哥ㄍㄜ說ㄕㄨㄛ：「快ㄎㄨㄞˋ起ㄑ一ˇ床ㄔㄨㄤˊ！準ㄓㄨㄣˇ備ㄅㄟˋ上ㄕㄤˋ學ㄒ一ㄝˊ了ㄌㄜ˙！」

我ㄨㄛˇ說ㄕㄨㄛ：「再ㄗㄞˋ一ㄧ分ㄈㄣ鐘ㄓㄨㄥ就ㄐ一ㄡˋ好ㄏㄠˇ啦ㄌㄚ。」

p.8-9

妹妹邊搖我邊說：「該醒來囉！」

我說：「走開啦！」

弟弟對著我的耳朵大叫：「起

來！起來！」

我大叫：「等一下嘛！」

p.10-11

爺爺喊著：「起床了！」

奶奶叫著：「起床！吃早餐了！」

爸爸大吼：「馬上給我起床！」

我說：「好啦，好啦！」

p.12-13

媽媽說：「快刷牙！」

姊姊說：「快洗臉！」

爸爸說：「穿上你的衣服！」

妹妹說：「快點吃早餐！」

p.14-15

哥哥說：「穿上鞋子！」

爺爺說：「穿上外套！」

弟弟說：「快去學校，別遲到了！」

p.16-17

姊姊大叫：「他忘記帶課本了！」

媽媽說：「你忘記帶課本了！」

爸爸說：「快點！你要遲到了！」

p.18-19

同學們大喊：「起來了！起來了！」

p.20-21

老師說:「快醒醒！要上數學課了!」

我的朋友說:「快醒醒！吃午餐了!」

p.22-23

校長說:「快醒醒！要打掃了!」

老師說:「快醒醒！要回家了!」

p.24-25

我大叫:「我醒了!」並一路跑回家。

p.31-32

1. Wake up!　　2. Brush your teeth!
3. Eat your breakfast!　　4. Put on your shoes!
5. You forgot your books!

英文課後練習

英文練習

　　小班又在賴床了！小朋友，請你一起幫忙叫小班起床，讓他能準時上學吧！下面有五張圖，請選出最適合這些情境的句子。

1

鬧鐘響了，可是小班還在睡覺！你知道這時候該對他說什麼嗎？

☐ Wash your face!
☐ Eat your breakfast!
☐ Wake up!

2

小班好不容易起床了，應該要刷牙囉！你知道該對他說哪一句話嗎？

☐ Go to school!
☐ Brush your teeth!
☐ Put on your coat!

③ 快快快！接下來小班該吃早餐了！哪一句才是正確的說法呢？

☐ Eat your breakfast!
☐ Wake up!
☐ Brush your teeth!

終於，小班吃完早餐要出門了。等等，鞋子呢？得叮嚀小班穿上鞋子才行！

④

☐ Get out of bed!
☐ Wash your face!
☐ Put on your shoes!

⑤ 糟糕，小班忘記拿課本了！趕快提醒他一下吧！

☐ You forgot your books!
☐ Go to school!
☐ Don't be late!

正確答案在第30頁喔！

童謠

　　小朋友，你是不是像故事裡的小班一樣會賴床呢？下面這首童謠，是關於上學前應該做的事。請跟著 CD Track 4 一起多唸幾次，學會這首童謠，下次你想賴床的時候，它就會提醒你「該起床啦！」

Time for School

上學啦！

Wakc up! Wake up! Time to get up!

The birds on the tree are singing morning song.

Brush your teeth and comb your hair,

Be ready for breakfast downstairs.

Take your bag and put on your hat,

Give your mommy a lovely kiss.

Look at the mirror and adjust your step,

Get up early and you'll never be late!

Kathleen R. Seaton is an Associate Professor in the Department of Foreign Languages and Literature at Tunghai University. She teaches a seminar course in Children's Literature, Film and Culture, courses in composition and oral practice and electives in acting and drama. She holds an interdisciplinary PhD in Mass Communication and an MFA in Film from Ohio University, Athens Ohio, U.S.A.

Kathleen R. Seaton （呂珍妮） 在東海大學外國語文學系擔任副教授。她教授兒童文學、電影與文化的文學討論課程，另外還開設英文作文和口語訓練兩堂主修課程，選修課程方面則有表演與戲劇。她擁有美國俄亥俄大學的大眾傳播學跨領域博士和電影藝術碩士學位。

寫書的人

　　姚紅畢業於南京藝術學院中國畫系，現職於江蘇少年兒童出版社，從事兒童繪本的編輯和創作多年。她的繪畫作品《蓬蓬頭溜冰的故事》獲第四屆中國優秀少年讀物一等獎；《牙印兒》獲國際兒童讀物聯盟「小松樹」獎；《飛吻大王》獲第五屆國家圖書獎。由姚紅策劃並與他人合作編輯的《「我真棒」幼兒成長圖畫書》獲 2000 年冰心兒童圖書獎。

畫畫的人

I Love My Family Series

我愛我的家系列

Kathleen R. Seaton 著／姚紅 繪

附中英雙語朗讀 CD
適讀對象：學習英文 0～2 年者（國小 1～3 年級適讀）

六本全新創作的中英雙語繪本，
六個溫馨幽默的故事，
帶領小朋友們進入單純可愛的小班的生活，
跟他一起分享和家人之間親密的感情！

Grandmother

Grandfather

Little Brother

Little Sister

Big Brother

Father

Mother

Ben

Big Sister

國家圖書館出版品預行編目資料

Wake Up! Wake Up!:起床了! / Kathleen R. Seaton
著;姚紅繪;本局編輯部譯.－－初版一刷.－－臺
北市：三民，2006
　　面；　　公分.－－(Fun心讀雙語叢書.我愛我的
　　家系列)
中英對照
ISBN 957–14–4247–X　　(精裝)

1. 英國語言－讀本

523.38　　　　　　　　　　　　　　94026450

網路書店位址　http://www.sanmin.com.tw

©　**Wake Up! Wake Up!**
起床了!

著作人　Kathleen R. Seaton
繪　者　姚　紅
譯　者　本局編輯部
發行人　劉振強
著作財
產權人　三民書局股份有限公司
　　　　臺北市復興北路386號
發行所　三民書局股份有限公司
　　　　地址 / 臺北市復興北路386號
　　　　電話 / (02)25006600
　　　　郵撥 / 0009998–5
印刷所　三民書局股份有限公司
門市部　復北店 / 臺北市復興北路386號
　　　　重南店 / 臺北市重慶南路一段61號
初版一刷　2006年1月
編　號　S 806041
定　價　新臺幣壹佰捌拾元整
行政院新聞局登記證局版臺業字第○二○○號

ISBN　957–14–4247–X　　(精裝)